DEREK

JETER

DEREK

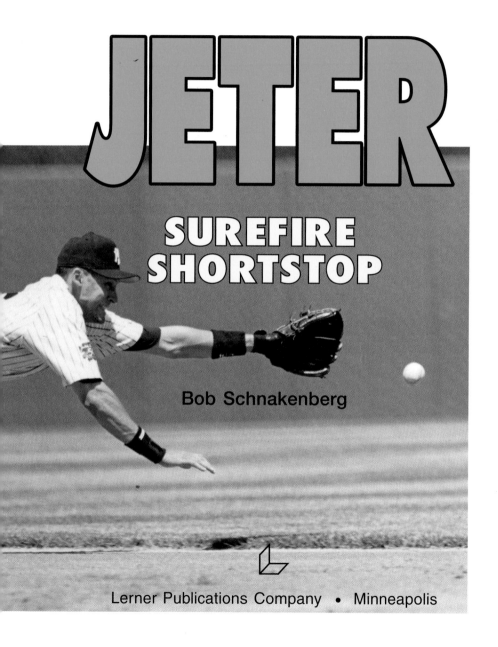

JETER

SUREFIRE SHORTSTOP

Bob Schnakenberg

Lerner Publications Company • Minneapolis

For my father. Thanks for everything.

The author would like to thank Jonathan Samet for his help in completing this book.

This book is available in two editions:
Library binding by Lerner Publications Company
Soft cover by First Avenue Editions
241 First Avenue North, Minneapolis, Minnesota 55401

Website address: www.lernerbooks.com

Library of Congress Cataloging-in-Publication Data

Schnakenberg, Robert.
    Derek Jeter : surefire shortstop / Bob Schnakenberg.
        p.   cm.
    Includes bibliographical references and index.
    Summary: Discusses the personal life and baseball career of the young man from Michigan who plays shortstop for the New York Yankees.
        ISBN 0–8225–3671–4 (alk. paper)—ISBN 0–8225–9838–8 (pbk. :alk. paper)
        1. Jeter, Derek, 1974– —Juvenile literature. 2. Baseball players—United States—Biography—Juvenile literature. [1. Jeter, Derek, 1974– 2. Baseball players. 3. Afro-Americans—Biography.] I. Title.
    GV865.J48S35   1999
    796.357'092—dc21
        [B]   98–8174

Manufactured in the United States of America
1 2 3 4 5 6 – JR – 04   03   02   01   00   99

Contents

Derek starts his pro career with a big hit in Cleveland.

A Tough Act to Follow

On Opening Day 1996, the Cleveland Indians met the New York Yankees' hot young shortstop, Derek Jeter (GEE tuhr). Derek grabbed their attention when he belted a long home run off Indians pitcher Dennis Martinez. That home run, Derek's first as a major leaguer, put the Yankees ahead of the defending American League champions, 2–0.

That was still the score in the bottom of the seventh inning when the Indians had two outs but a runner on second. A ground ball, fielded correctly, could end the Indians' chance to score. A base hit could cut the Yankees' lead in half and chase their best pitcher from the game.

As Yankees ace David Cone went into his pitching motion, the runner on second dashed for third. The batter, Indians shortstop Omar Vizquel, lifted a fly ball into shallow left field by outfielder Gerald Williams.

A rookie in 1996, Derek was more than a little nervous about being in the big leagues.

Williams stormed in, but he had been way back. He wouldn't be able to make the catch. *It's a hit,* Cone thought in disgust. *It's 2–1, and I'm out of the game.*

But Derek, the Yankees' rookie shortstop, had gotten a lightning jump on the ball. With his back toward home plate, he sprinted into leftfield. Keeping his eye on the floating baseball as it danced in the wind above him, he lunged and caught the ball over his left shoulder. "I kept running and running," Derek said of the play, "and then I got to it. I just made up my mind I wanted the ball hit to me."

The diving backhand catch ended the inning and the Indians' rally. The Yankee **bullpen,** led by hard-throwing **closer** John Wetteland, then sealed the Yankee victory. After the game, Cone said, "That was a major league play. I think right then and there, we all learned something about Derek."

The rest of major league baseball learned about Derek over the course of the 1996 season. As a child, Derek had dreamed of playing shortstop for the Yankees. With confidence and determination, he achieved that dream. Tall, powerful, and smart, Derek impressed fans and players alike throughout the 162–game season, which ended with the Yankees claiming their first world championship in 18 years. Derek was voted American League Rookie of the Year and slipped on a World Series ring, all before his 22nd birthday. Not bad for a kid from Kalamazoo.

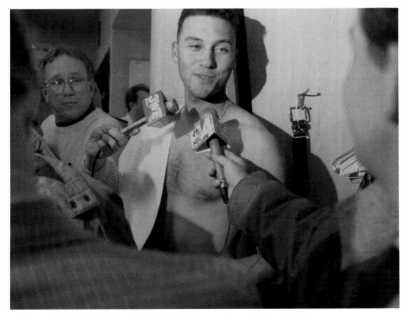

After Derek helped the Yankees beat the Indians, everyone wanted to know about New York's new shortstop.

As a Little Leaguer, Derek had big dreams.

2

A Kid from Kalamazoo

Rising at the crack of dawn on a warm summer morning, little Derek Jeter had one thing on his mind—baseball. Derek, his sister, Sharlee, and their cousins spent the summer months at their grandmother's house. She lived in West Milford, a town in northern New Jersey that wasn't far from New York City. All of his cousins were still sleeping, but Derek knew he had a partner for playing catch.

"C'mon, Gram, let's throw!" Derek said to his grandmother, Dot Connors. Most summer mornings, Dot would follow him out into the yard to play catch. Even as a little child, Derek threw the ball so hard he almost knocked his grandmother over.

Derek had been born June 26, 1974, in West Milford. His family moved to Kalamazoo, Michigan, when Derek was four. Derek's father, Charles Jeter, worked as a drug and alcohol counselor in Kalamazoo. Derek's mother, Dorothy Jeter, was an accountant. His sister Sharlee, five years younger than Derek, also played ball. Charles and Dorothy always tried to go to their children's games.

At first, Derek wanted to be a pitcher. But he soon set his sights on becoming a shortstop instead. His father had been a shortstop in college. Derek's father would often spend hours with him, leafing through the scrapbook he kept from his playing days. "If you become a good player, you'll get your own scrapbook one day," Charles told his son.

Those conversations made a strong impression on Derek. "When you're young, you want to be like your dad," Derek later said. Derek had inherited his father's athletic ability, especially the quickness and hand-eye coordination that are so important in playing shortstop.

Charles Jeter taught his son about all the skills of baseball. "I wanted him to be an all-round player," Derek's dad said. "I would tell him, 'You have to have more range if you want to play shortstop.' " He meant that Derek had to improve his quickness to be able to catch balls that were hit "in the hole" between shortstop and second base.

Derek and Sharlee, along with their parents, would jump the fence that separated their backyard from the baseball field at Kalamazoo Central High School. Then Derek would position himself at shortstop while his family members took turns hitting ground balls to him.

Derek's family: father Charles, sister Sharlee, and mother Dorothy.

Sharlee and Derek were both athletic as youngsters.

"Derek had goals," recalled his mother, "but he knew if he wanted to play in the Little League all-star game or go to baseball camp, he better come home with a 4.0 [grade point average], he better have his behavior intact and he better make curfew or he wasn't going anywhere." The Jeters even made Derek sign a contract every year, spelling out what they expected from him in school and in athletics. The contracts helped Derek focus on meeting his goals.

Derek played second base for his Little League baseball team and dreamed about playing in the major leagues. As he got older, his dream focused on the New York Yankees. Derek visited Yankee Stadium during his summers with his grandmother in New Jersey. He cheered for Yankee stars such as Dave Winfield, Don Mattingly, and Ron Guidry.

Before Derek was even out of Little League, he told his father that he wanted to be the starting shortstop for the New York Yankees when he grew up. Charles and Dorothy Jeter knew they had raised their son to be confident, not cocky. "In our house, you couldn't go around talking about yourself," Derek said. The Jeters knew that Derek was setting a goal for himself. The whole family rallied around to help him pursue his dream.

When Derek was in sixth grade, his Aunt Julie gave him a gold New York Yankees necklace as a present. Along with a blue Yankees windbreaker that he wore constantly, this medallion soon became his prized possession. Photographs of Derek in his Yankee jackets and jerseys began popping up in frames on the walls of the Jeter home in Kalamazoo. Derek was so sure that he was born to wear the pinstripes—a key part of the Yankees' uniform—that he had it noted in his eighth grade yearbook. In 10 years, said the caption under his photo, he would be playing for the New York Yankees.

Dave Winfield, one of Derek's favorite players, once wore the pinstriped uniform of the New York Yankees.

At Kalamazoo Central High School, Derek was an A student and a power-hitting shortstop on the baseball team. By the time he was in high school, Derek had discovered that girls could be almost as fascinating as baseball. They liked him, too. Tall and handsome with piercing green eyes, he found himself the center of attention for something other than his base-ball skills. "Girls would call here all the time," his mother remembers.

Still, Derek kept focused on his athletic goals. He also played basketball in high school, and he always wanted to take the game-winning shot. But baseball remained Derek's passion. His idol was Barry Larkin, the former University of Michigan star who played for the Cincinnati Reds. Like Derek, Larkin was a short-stop who could hit for power.

Derek enjoys a school dance with a girlfriend.

Derek was a versatile athlete in high school.

In Derek's junior year of high school, he had a scorching **batting average** of .557. As a senior, his average remained high at .508. The American Baseball Coaches Association named Derek the 1992 High School Player of the Year. He was beginning to look like a great prospect for the major league baseball draft. Each spring, the professional teams take turns selecting the most promising young players in the country. Sometimes, the teams and players sign contracts and the players join the professional team's system of minor league teams.

By the end of his senior year, scouts from 27 of the 28 major league baseball clubs had contacted Derek.

Derek hit better than .500 in his junior and senior years.

Cincinnati shortstop Barry Larkin played baseball the way Derek wanted to play the game.

They all wanted him to play on their team. Only one team had not talked to him—the Yankees! "I was wondering why they were the only team that didn't call," he said. As draft day approached, Derek heard a rumor that the Cincinnati Reds would pick him. His idol Barry Larkin was the Reds' shortstop. Derek feared he would be stuck in a backup role, but he had no say in which team chose him.

Two days before the draft, a Yankee scout phoned him. The scout said the Yankees had been following his progress for the previous two years. The Yankees had not contacted him because they didn't want to disturb his family's privacy.

The scout said the Yankees might pick Derek if he were available when their turn came in the draft. Derek was glad the Yankees were interested in him but New York was scheduled to pick just after Cincinnati in the draft. Derek began picturing himself in a Reds uniform.

On draft day, Derek waited anxiously. When the Reds' turn came, they decided to choose outfielder Chad Mottola, who had already proven himself in college. The Yankees could pick Derek. Soon, Derek's phone rang. A Yankee official was on the other end of the line. Derek had been the Yankees' first pick in the 1992 draft. He was the sixth player chosen in the country.

Before Derek signed a contract with the Yankees, he asked the team to pay for his college education. Derek's parents were both successful professionals. They knew that education was important for Derek's future after baseball. A college degree would also help him if he was injured and had to quit playing baseball. Derek's parents wanted him to have a chance for college, no matter how long it might take him to earn his degree. Yankees owner George Steinbrenner agreed to Derek's request, and Derek signed a $700,000 contract to play for the Yankees. It seemed like the conclusion of a beautiful dream. But the dream was only beginning.

The Yankee Keeper

The Yankees sent Derek to their Rookie League minor league team in Tampa, Florida. If Derek did well in the Gulf Coast League, he would be promoted to Class AA, or even to Class AAA, the last step before the majors. Although Derek entered professional baseball with a good attitude, things did not go according to his plan. He struggled offensively, hitting only around .200. In the field, he was even worse. Derek made 21 **errors** in 58 games—way too many for a starting shortstop. Even worse, he was so homesick he spent more than $300 a month in long-distance phone calls to his family. After every bad game, his parents talked to him, stressing the good things to keep his confidence from sagging.

The following spring, Derek packed his bags and headed for North Carolina. The Yankees had assigned him to the Greensboro Hornets of the South Atlantic

League. The Yankees hoped that a full year playing in this Class A league would allow Derek to develop his skills to their fullest.

Again, Derek began 1993, his first full season as a pro, with a positive attitude. He was confident that he could hit and he was determined to improve his fielding. "Defense comes first as a shortstop," he said. "Hitting is an extra." This time Derek did hit well but he still struggled to field his position.

"I was making errors every day," he said. His poor defensive play affected his confidence. "I was saying 'Maybe they won't hit another ground ball to shortstop,' and it was only the first two weeks of the season."

Fresh out of high school and on his own in the minor leagues, Derek often got homesick.

At midnight on game nights, the phone in the Jeter house would ring. Charles and Dorothy Jeter would look at each other with knowing smiles. "Mom, you take this one," Charles would say to his wife. It was Derek calling from Greensboro to talk about another disappointing night at shortstop. The Jeters would ask Derek what he had done wrong. They would suggest ways he could correct the problem. Then, they would give him the best advice of all: Forget about the errors and move on. "You have to go from game to game," Derek's dad would say. "You can't let your game fall apart because of one bad play."

Derek's defensive struggles continued throughout the 1993 season. He finished the year with 56 errors in 128 games. It was much too high a total for a starting shortstop. At the plate, however, Derek had batted .295, the fifth highest average in the Yankee organization. Among his 152 hits were 14 doubles, 11 triples, and 5 home runs. Once on base, Derek was a nuisance to opposing teams, swiping 18 bases in 27 tries. For his offensive skills, the managers of the South Atlantic League named him their Most Outstanding Major League Prospect. *Baseball America,* a magazine that covers the minor leagues, called him the most exciting player in the minors. Even better for Derek's confidence, the magazine also honored him as the top defensive shortstop, despite his high error total. The baseball experts—as well as the Yankee organization—continued to predict that he would develop into an outstanding player.

Derek's first stop on the road to that goal was the Fall Instructional League in Tampa. In this special camp, young players work with coaches to improve the weak areas of their game. Derek's tutor was Yankee coach Brian Butterfield. Derek's physical makeup, especially his size and arm strength, impressed Coach Butterfield. He disagreed with some scouts who suggested moving Derek to third base or the outfield. "It looks like he's going to be a pretty big guy," Butterfield observed, "but his athleticism is going to allow him to be a shortstop. He has quick feet, and they're going to get quicker as he matures."

Derek's willingness to improve as a fielder also impressed Butterfield. "I think a lot of my errors were trying to do too much," Derek admitted. "I was doing a lot of unneeded motion, things that were affecting the way I handled ground balls." To correct these problems, Butterfield helped Derek concentrate on the basics, like positioning. Butterfield showed him how to field the ball in his throwing position. That way, Derek didn't have to bring his glove across his body and he wouldn't end up tripping over his own feet.

Derek's focus on fielding paid off almost right away. In 20 games in the Fall Instructional League, he made only one error. In the spring of 1994, he was invited to the Yankees' major league spring training camp in Fort Lauderdale, Florida. The Yankees weren't going to move their talented teenager to the majors so soon, but they wanted him to get a taste of life in big league surroundings.

Yankees manager Buck Showalter liked what he saw in Derek. "He came into big league camp with a certain respect," said Showalter. "But at the same time, he was not intimidated by the pace of the game, the athleticism of it." The Yankees timed all their players in the 60-yard dash. Derek finished in the top five.

Derek worked on his fielding in the minor leagues to develop the smooth moves he uses with the Yankees.

New York manager Buck Showalter gave Derek his first chance with the Yankees.

As the 1994 season opener neared, the Yankees had a decision to make. They could send Derek back to Tampa, where he had struggled two seasons earlier, or they could push him up to the Class AA team in up-state New York. "You don't want to push a kid too soon and see him fail," said Coach Butterfield. "At the same time, if he's ready to take the next step you want to do it as soon as possible."

The Yankees chose to be cautious with their top prospect. They assigned him to Tampa. Before long, Derek forced them to rethink their decision. He hit .329 in 69 games in Tampa, earning Florida League

MVP honors in less than half a season. The Yankees moved him to their Class AA team in Albany, New York. But the Class AA level proved even less of a challenge for the rapidly blossoming shortstop. Derek hit at a .377 clip in 34 games at Albany and was named Eastern League Player of the Month for July. Most important, his fielding had improved. His errors were no longer a problem.

The minor league field in Albany, New York, isn't nearly as fancy as Yankee Stadium in the Bronx.

The Yankees promoted Derek again, this time to their Class AAA team in Columbus, Ohio. On August 1, Derek's mother drove from Kalamazoo to watch Derek play his first game for the Columbus Clippers. Her son was one step away from the major leagues!

However, the major league players weren't playing. A players' strike against the major league baseball owners, over salaries and other issues, cut short the 1994 season. Since the Yankees were no longer playing, the team sent manager Buck Showalter to watch Derek play at Columbus. Showalter was as impressed as he had been in spring training.

"He'd fit right into our clubhouse," said Showalter, after seeing the way Derek got along with his teammates and coaches. Derek finished out the season by hitting .349 in 35 Class AAA games. For the year, he made only 25 errors in 138 games on three minor league levels. His batting average of .344 prompted *Baseball America* to name him Minor League Player of the Year.

With such a promising rookie waiting to take over at shortstop, Yankee fans couldn't wait for Opening Day in 1995. But Derek had injured his shoulder while playing in the Arizona Fall League, and the Yankees decided not to rush him into the major leagues. Instead, Derek found himself back in Columbus, Ohio. He continued to play well, waiting for his chance to prove he belonged in the big leagues.

By working hard in the minor leagues, Derek earned the award for the Player of the Year.

That chance finally came in May of 1995. Injuries to starting shortstop Tony Fernandez and second baseman Pat Kelly left the Yankees with holes in their infield. On May 29, they filled one of those holes by bringing Derek to the majors.

Derek jokes with his good friend and rival shortstop,
Alex Rodriguez of the Seattle Mariners.

Shortstop of the Future

The Kingdome in Seattle can scare even the most seasoned major leaguer. The high roof with its hanging loudspeakers makes it easy to lose sight of a pop fly. The crowd noise has been known to rattle the nerves of even veteran visiting players. And the Kingdome was where Derek would play his first game as a New York Yankee.

Derek's dad got up at three o'clock on the morning of Derek's first game. Charles Jeter flew from Kalamazoo to be in the stands that night in Seattle. Derek's mother stayed home so that she could go to Sharlee's high school softball game. Derek understood. "She's just as important as I am," he said. "Why would they want to see only me?" All through the game, a television crew trained its camera on Charles's reactions to his son's debut. It was the first of many nail-biting nights for the Jeter family.

Derek made a couple of outstanding defensive plays in his first game, but he struggled at the plate. He had no hits in five **at bats.** Worst of all, Derek struck out swinging in the 11th inning with the **go-ahead run** on third. The Mariners went on to win 8–7 in 12 innings.

Striking out always frustrates Derek.

As Derek's fielding improved, his playing time increased.

Derek started the next 13 games at shortstop. He made only two errors and batted .234 with six **runs batted in (RBIs).** Despite his solid performance, he was sent back down to the minors on June 12. The return of regular shortstop Tony Fernandez, who was uncomfortable playing second base, meant the Yankees had too many shortstops. Derek took the decision in stride. "I'll be back eventually," he said.

Derek warms up before a Yankee game.

"Eventually" turned out to be in September. The Yankees expanded their roster to 40 players then and called Derek back up from Columbus. Derek didn't get to play much that fall, but he did have a great view of the **pennant** race. The Yankees played outstanding baseball over the final month to lock up an American League playoff spot. For the first time in 14 years, the Yankees were back in the playoffs! But the season ended for Derek and his teammates in the first round. They lost to Seattle in a hard-fought five-game playoff series.

Yankee fans looked toward the 1996 season with great expectations. Over the winter, the club had hired a new manager, former Cardinal great Joe Torre. The Yankees also had signed some new players in an effort to build on the successes of 1995. Long before the season started, Torre announced that Derek would be the team's starting shortstop. The decision put an awful lot of pressure on Derek, but he knew his new manager believed in him.

Joe Torre took over as the manager of the Yankees before the 1996 season.

Derek is big and he knows when to hustle.

Derek spent the winter in Tampa, working out at the team's minor-league training center. For nearly four months, he worked out every day. He added 10 pounds of muscle onto his slight frame to stand at 6 feet 3 inches and 185 pounds. He wanted to get stronger to keep from becoming tired during the six-month major league season.

Manager Joe Torre wasn't expecting much from his new shortstop. Even though Derek had some major league experience, he was officially considered a rookie. He would be playing the most important in-field position in a city with a history of great short-stops, from the Yankee great Phil Rizzuto to the Brooklyn Dodger legend Pee Wee Reese. Torre knew the pressure on Derek would be tremendous. "If he hits .240 or .250 and makes the plays, I'll be happy," Torre said.

Quite a surprise lay in store for Torre on Opening Day in Cleveland. He might have known something was up when Derek strode past him in the dugout be-fore the game. "Are you ready?" the untested rookie said to the manager with more than 30 years of pro baseball experience. A smile came to Torre's face. *So far, so good,* he thought to himself.

That day, Torre watched as his confident young shortstop led the Yanks to victory with his home run and over-the-shoulder catch. The following night, Derek clubbed three hits and scored three runs as the Yankees again trounced Cleveland, 5–1. Dorothy Jeter was in the stands for both games. Meanwhile, Charles was watching Sharlee's softball opener back at Kalamazoo Central.

It was the beginning of a dream season for the Yankees. Under the steady hand of Joe Torre, the team's blend of young players and talented veterans produced a string of memorable victories. On April 29 in Baltimore, the Yankees fell behind 9–4 to their division rivals, the Orioles, but came back to win, 13–10, in one of the longest baseball games ever played. The players stood in the field so long that Baltimore's Brady Anderson had to change his shoes to relieve his aching feet.

On a warm May night at Yankee Stadium, Yankees pitcher Dwight Gooden held the powerful Seattle Mariners lineup without a hit through $8^2/_3$ innings. Two walks in the ninth put Seattle runners on second and third. Then Gooden bore down. He got power-hitting Paul Sorrento to chase a high **curveball** and pop it into short leftfield. The crowd froze in anticipation for what seemed like an eternity. Then the ball landed in Derek's waiting glove. He squeezed it closed, and Gooden had the 11th **no-hitter** in Yankee history! Gooden's triumphant teammates carried him off the field in celebration. After victories like this one, the Yankees began to believe they could win their division—and perhaps the world championship.

Derek's batting average was .314 during the 1996 season.

Always a favorite with fans, Derek signs lots of autographs.

As spring gave way to summer, the Yankees continued to ride atop the American League East standings. Sportswriters stopped writing about Derek's hot start and started writing about his consistent fine play. Of course, there were bumps along the way. During one game in Chicago, Derek tried to steal third base in the eighth inning of a tie game, with slugger Cecil Fielder batting. He was thrown out, which ended the Yankee rally and angered Joe Torre. As the steaming manager took deep breaths to try to calm himself down, Derek sat down beside him in the dugout.

"What are you doing?" Torre asked.

"I'm coming to you so you can yell at me and get it over with," answered Derek.

The Yankees' division lead shrank to two games in September. A late-summer slump and a strong drive by the Baltimore Orioles kept the pressure on New York. But on September 25, the Yankees clinched the American League East by defeating the Milwaukee Brewers. The Yankees would be in the playoffs.

The Yankees played the Texas Rangers in the first round of the playoffs. The Rangers boasted a powerful lineup, led by slugger Juan Gonzalez and competitive catcher Ivan "Pudge" Rodriguez. But the Yankees, with their solid pitching and playoff experience, went into the series as a heavy favorite.

Texas surprised New York by taking the first game at Yankee Stadium, 6–2. Derek had only one hit in four at bats, and he left several runners on base. Some New York newspapers began to doubt whether Derek and the Yankees could win. But Joe Torre stayed confident in his club and his shortstop.

"The difference about the postseason is that you still want to lean on experienced guys," the manager said. "To me, Jeter is different. I've been around a lot of young kids and a lot of rookies. He's done a lot of growing up this year. He doesn't see the postseason as something different."

Derek rewarded the faith of his manager in the second playoff game, which went into extra innings. He led off the 12th inning with a single. He later scored the winning run on an error by Ranger third baseman Dean Palmer. In the third game, in Texas, Derek started the winning rally with a hit in the ninth inning. In the fourth game, he drove in a run to help the Yankees come from behind to win. Derek and the Yankees went home with a three-games-to-one series victory.

Next up for the Yanks was an American League Championship Series matchup against the Orioles. Again, Derek was at the center of the action.

The Orioles were leading, 4–3, in the eighth inning of the opener at Yankee Stadium, when Derek sent a long fly ball into rightfield. Oriole outfielder Tony Tarasco backed up against the fence to try to catch it, but a 12-year-old boy stuck his glove out and snatched it away from him. The ball bounced off the boy's mitt and into the stands for a home run. The Yankees then won the game in extra innings on a home run by Bernie Williams.

After the Orioles evened the series, Derek started the winning rally with a key double in the third game in Baltimore. From that point on, the Yankees took over. Derek fielded the final out of the championship series, throwing out Cal Ripken from deep in the hole at shortstop. The Yankees were in the World Series!

Derek steps on second base to force out Todd Zeile.

In the World Series, the Yankees would play the National League champion Atlanta Braves. The Braves were the defending world champions. They boasted the best pitching staff in baseball, led by Greg Maddux and John Smoltz. Most baseball experts thought the first two games at Yankee Stadium would be the key to the series. If the Yankees could win on their home field, they might stand a chance against the favored Braves. But if New York dropped even one of the opening contests, the Braves would be almost impossible to beat.

Things went bad from the start for New York. In Game One, Smoltz was brilliant, limiting the Yankees to one run on two hits over six innings. The Braves cruised to a 12–1 victory. The second game was no better for the Yankees. With Maddux throwing just 82 pitches, Atlanta made short work of New York, 4–0.

The losses were painful for Derek in more ways than one. In the third inning of Game Two, a pitch from Maddux hit Derek's left wrist. He crumpled to the ground in pain before continuing in the game. X rays after the game showed no broken bones.

Derek had five hits during the World Series.

On October 23, Derek and the Yankees knew what a challenging task they had before them in Atlanta. They would have to win four of the final five games of the Series. The first three of these games would be in Atlanta's home park.

Before Game Three, Manager Torre told the Yankees to try to score early against Braves starting pitcher Tom Glavine. Glavine got better as a game went on, Torre said, so the Yankees would have to strike first. Derek did just that. His **sacrifice bunt** in the top of the first inning helped the Yanks to their first lead in the Series. New York held onto the lead and won, 5–2.

In Game Four, the Yankees were down 6–0, but they came back to win after tying the game in the eighth inning on a home run by Jim Leyritz. The Series was tied at two wins each for the Yankees and the Braves, with one more game in Atlanta. In Game Five, Yankee starting pitcher Andy Pettitte and his teammates eked out a 1–0 win.

The World Series returned to Yankee Stadium for Game Six. The New York fans cheered their lungs out for what could be the team's first championship since 1978. Once again, the Yankees faced Braves pitcher Greg Maddux, who had dominated them in Game Two of the Series. This time, however, his pitches were not quite so sharp. Slugger Paul O'Neill doubled to open the Yankees' third inning.

Derek cheers as New York puts out another Brave.

After a ground ball out, catcher Joe Girardi crushed a long triple into centerfield and O'Neill scored the game's first run. That brought Derek to the plate, with one out and Girardi on third. Derek knocked in Girardi with a hard single. Then Derek stole second and scored on a single by Bernie Williams.

The Yankees' 3–0 lead was trimmed to 3–2 by the Braves' offense. In the ninth inning, Atlanta got a runner on base with two outs. But the next batter, Mark Lemke, popped up a foul near the third-base line that settled into Charlie Hayes's glove. Derek could barely contain his excitement as he watched the final play. "I wanted to push Charlie out of the way and catch it," he said after the game.

The Yankees fell into a pile on the infield to celebrate their amazing World Series triumph. The mass of players eventually formed a line and took a victory lap around Yankee Stadium. The 50,000 fans in the stadium roared as their heroes thanked them for a wonderful season. "We just floated," said David Cone. "Guys jumping up and down...It was an incredible feeling. We were floating."

In his first year in the majors, Derek had achieved every baseball player's fondest dream. "That's by far the best experience I've had playing baseball," he said of the World Series victory.

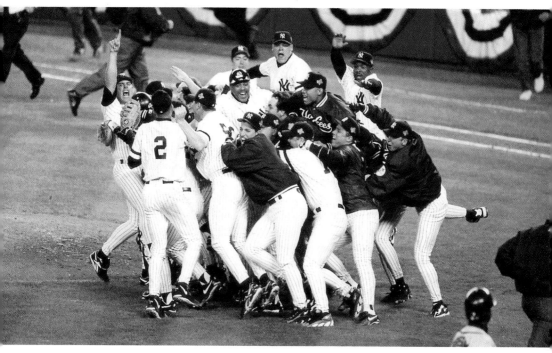

Yankees flood the field after winning the World Series.

New York City held a huge parade for its champions.

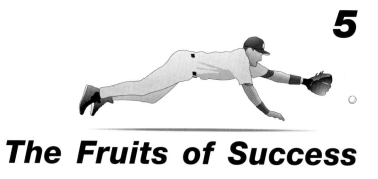

The Fruits of Success

It rarely snows in New York City before Christmas. But on an October afternoon in 1996, a blizzard of confetti fell on what New Yorkers call the "Canyon of Heroes." Residents of the city had gathered before to witness parades on this street, honoring Pope John Paul II, Nelson Mandela, and the veterans of the Persian Gulf War. But this particular day belonged to the New York Yankees.

Derek and the other World Series champions rode on floats that day. Dressed smartly in a black leather jacket, beside his teammates Cecil Fielder and Bernie Williams, Derek waved and smiled at the millions of fans lining the streets. New York's mayor and Yankee manager Joe Torre gave speeches to the crowd after the parade. That evening, Derek and a few of the players dropped by the television studio where *The Late Show with David Letterman* was being broadcast.

On November 5, 1996, Derek learned he had been unanimously selected the American League's Rookie of the Year. His .314 average, 10 home runs, and 78 RBIs made the decision an easy one for the baseball writers who give out the award. "I've got to give credit to my teammates," Derek said. "I got a lot of RBIs, but they got on base. I just got lucky."

For Charles Jeter, the award was the product of hard work, not luck. "I feel tremendous pride in him," said Derek's father. "I'm proud that he accomplished something that he wanted."

When the hoopla surrounding the 1996 season died down, Derek began looking forward to the next baseball season. Before he began training for 1997, he had one other task he wanted to perform.

Derek had always hoped to be able to start his own charitable foundation, just like his favorite Yankee, Dave Winfield. In December 1996, Derek started the Turn 2 Foundation, an organization designed to steer kids away from drugs and alcohol. To help run Turn 2, Derek turned to someone who had years of experience in the field—his father. As an experienced drug counselor, Charles directs Turn 2's activities in schools, rehabilitation centers, and hospitals. Derek visits schools and speaks to kids about the importance of staying in school. With Derek as president, the Jeters operate the foundation out of Kalamazoo, Michigan.

Once Turn 2 was established, Derek could again concentrate on baseball. He headed for Tampa, Florida, and began practicing and training with weights. He was determined to improve on his rookie season.

The 1997 season was another successful one for Derek and the Yankees. They did not repeat as division champions, but they won 95 games and made the play-offs for the third straight year. Derek got off to a hot start but slumped at mid-season. But he rebounded strongly after the **All-Star break** and finished the year hitting .291 with 10 home runs and 70 RBIs.

Derek tries to help kids with his Turn 2 Foundation.

Two lucky Little Leaguers get to stand with Derek during the national anthem before a Yankees game.

In the first game of the playoffs against Cleveland, Derek hit the second of three consecutive Yankee home runs for a dramatic come-from-behind New York victory. But the Yankees lost the series to the Indians, three games to two.

For Derek, 1997 was a successful year off the field. The Turn 2 Foundation raised $305,000 in donations in its first year and began planning to expand to New York.

Derek lent his time to the cause by meeting with 750 young people from western Michigan who had stayed clear of drugs and performed well in school.

During the baseball season, Derek lives in an apartment in New York City. He also bought a house in Tampa, Florida, near the Yankees' minor league training facility, so he could continue to work out in the winter. His mother took time off from her job to decorate his new home at holiday time. All the Jeters got together to celebrate Christmas in Derek's new home.

Derek continues to improve his skills at shortstop.

What sets Derek apart from many other young superstars are the strong values he brings to his personal life. "Baseball is the easy part," he has said. "Off the field is when people look up to you even more. That's when your job starts." With that in mind, at holiday time, Derek visits sick patients in the children's ward at Bronson Hospital in Kalamazoo, Michigan. At games, he signs autographs for his fans and often stops to chat with the folks in the front row.

Derek recruits other celebrities, including gymnast Dominique Dawes and outfielder Gerald Williams, to help with Turn 2 activities.

As a grown-up, Derek went back to his old school to talk to youngsters who look up to him.

Such attention might go to another man's head—but not Derek's. He keeps a sense of balance about his growing fame. "I have a regular life," he says. "I think I'm no different than anyone else. It's just a job I do. Other than that, I think I'm just as normal as any other person."

In many ways, Derek Jeter has lived a fairytale life. He has achieved many of his dreams at an early age without losing his sense of values. Does it ever feel like it's too much too soon? "No," he says. "If it's too much too soon, I hope I get too much every year."

Career Highlights

Minor Leagues

Year	Team/League	G	AB	R	H	AVG.	SB	PO	A	E
1992	Yankees/Gulf Coast	47	173	19	35	.202	2	67	132	12
1992	Greensboro/South Atlantic	11	37	4	9	.243	0	14	25	9
1993	Greensboro/South Atlantic	128	515	85	152	.295	18	158	292	56
1994	Tampa/Florida State	69	292	61	96	.329	28	93	204	12
1994	Albany/Eastern	34	122	17	46	.377	12	42	105	6
1994	Columbus/International	35	126	25	44	.349	10	54	93	7
1995	Columbus/International	123	486	96	154	.317	20	189	394	29
	Totals	447	1,751	307	536	.306	90	617	1,245	131

Major Leagues

Year	Team/League	G	AB	R	H	AVG.	SB	PO	A	E
1995	Yankees/American	15	48	5	12	.250	0	17	34	2
1996	Yankees/American	157	582	104	183	.314	14	244	444	22
1997	Yankees/American	159	654	116	190	.290	23	245	457	18
*1998	Yankees/American	69	297	62	94	.316	15	108	219	4
	Totals	400	1,581	287	479	.303	52	614	1,154	46

*—through All-Star break
G=Games played, AB=At Bats, R=Runs scored, H=Hits, AVG.=Batting average,
SB=Stolen bases, PO=Put-outs, A=Assists, E=Errors

- American League All Star, 1998
- American League Rookie of the Year, 1996
- Minor League Player of the Year, 1994
- Florida State League Most Valuable Player, 1994
- Florida State League All Star, 1994
- Topps Class A All Star, 1994
- South Atlantic League All Star, 1993
- Voted Most Outstanding Major League Prospect by South Atlantic League managers, 1993
- Signed by New York in the first round (sixth pick overall) of the 1992 draft
- Named High School Player of the Year by the American Baseball Coaches Association, 1992

Glossary

All-Star break: The four-day period in July when major league teams take a break for the annual All-Star Game.

at bats: Official attempts to hit a pitched ball. Hitting a sacrifice, being walked, or being hit by a pitch doesn't count as an at bat.

batting average: The number of hits a batter gets, divided by the batter's official at bats, carried to three decimal places. For example, if Derek gets 30 hits in 90 at bats, his batting average is .333.

bullpen: Pitchers who replace the starting pitchers. These pitchers sit in an area next to the outfield so that they can warm up when the manager tells them they will be needed. The area in which they sit is also called the bullpen.

closer: The pitcher who comes in to pitch the last inning or two.

curveball: A pitch that is thrown so that it spins and moves downward and to the right or left of the batter.

errors: Mistakes by a fielder that result in a batter or baserunner reaching a base safely.

go-ahead run: A run that breaks a tie.

no-hitter: A game in which the pitcher does not allow the opposing team a base hit.

pennant: The American League championship and the National League championship in Major League Baseball. The league champions then go on to play one another in the World Series.

run batted in (RBI): A run that is scored as a result of a batter getting a hit or, if the bases are loaded, the batter drawing a walk.

sacrifice bunt: An intentionally soft hit when a runner is on first base. The bunt lands somewhere between the catcher and the pitcher. The fielders usually throw to first base to put out the batter, but the baserunner moves to second. The batter has sacrificed himself or herself to advance the runner.

Sources

Information for this book was obtained from the following sources: Interview with Veromica Webb; Mel Antonen (*USA Today*, 5 November 1996); Jack Canfora (*People*, 12 May 1997); Jack Curry (*The New York Times*, 24 December 1997); Bob Klapisch (*The Sporting News*, 29 April 1996)' David Lennon (*Newsday*, 16 March 1997); Tom Pedulla (*Gannett News Service*, 22 March 1994); Gary Teubner (*ESPN Sports Zone*, 26 December 1997); Kelly Whiteside (*Sports Illustrated*, 13 November 1996); Lisa Winston (*Baseball Weekly*, 2 September 1994).

Index

Write to Derek:

You can send mail to Derek at the address on the right. If you write a letter, don't get your hopes up too high. Derek and other athletes get lots of letters every day, and they aren't always able to answer them all.

Derek Jeter
c/o The New York Yankees
Yankee Stadium
161st St. & River Ave.
Bronx, NY 10451

Acknowledgments ·

Photographs are reproduced with the permission of: SportsChrome East/West, John Klein, p. 1; Reuters/Mike Segar/Archive Photos, pp. 2–3; Reuters/Ron Kuntz/Archive Photos, p. 6; Jim Merihew/Kalamazoo Gazette, pp. 8, 9, 13; Turn 2 Foundation, Inc., pp. 10, 14, 53; Sports-Chrome East/West, pp. 16, 28, 38, 41, 46; Seth Poppel Yearbook Archives, pp. 17, 18, 19, 24; © John Klein, pp. 20, 32, 35, 37; The Greensboro Bats, p. 22; Times Union/Albany, N.Y., p. 29; AP/Wide World Photos, pp. 31, 62; © ALLSPORT USA/Elsa Hasch, p. 34; Bob Falcetti/Tampa Tribune, p. 36; © ALLSPORT USA/Stephen Dunn, p. 42; © ALLSPORT USA/Doug Pensinger, p. 45; SportsChrome East/West, Rob Tringali, Jr., pp. 27, 48, 49, 54; © ALLSPORT USA/Thomas Hinton, p. 50; Agence France Presse/Corbis-Bettmann, p. 55; Don Campbell/Kalamazoo Gazette, p. 56; Shelley Eades/Kalamazoo Gazette, p. 57; © John SooHoo/Endzone, p. 59.

Front cover and back cover photographs by © John Klein.
Artwork by Michael Tacheny.

About the Author

A life-long sports fan, Bob Schnakenberg is an accomplished author of reference and educational materials for children and adults. His past credits include *The Grolier Library of International Biographies*, Lerner Publication Company's *Scottie Pippen, Reluctant Superstar*, and the CD-ROM movie guide *Microsoft Cinemania*.